Hawks

written and illustrated by

Charles L. Ripper

WILLIAM MORROW & COMPANY

New York, 1956

To my mother and father

Grateful recognition is given to Dr. Kenneth C. Parkes, Associate Curator of Birds, Carnegie Museum, Pittsburgh, Pennsylvania, for reading and criticizing the manuscript.

· · · · ·

For centuries the hawk has been known as the king of hunters in the bird world. Hawks and many of their relatives are noted for powerful flight, courage and strength, and keen sight. That is why people have often chosen hawks as symbols of their own strength and courage. The bald eagle, a close relative of the hawk, is, of course, the emblem of the United States of America. Ancient peoples also used hawks as symbols. Roman legionaries displayed the

eagle on their standards and Norsemen wore
hawk wings on their helmets. American In-
dians used hawk and eagle feathers on their
war bonnets to show victories over their enemies.

Different species of hawks and their relatives
are found in almost every country in the world.
Falcons, rough-legged hawks, kites, harriers,
caracaras, and ospreys are some of the birds
that belong to the hawk family. In America

most of these birds are simply called hawks. Vultures are also closely related to this group, although sometimes they are not included in it.

Hawks differ greatly in size. Some of our North American hawks have a wingspread of more than four feet; others are not much larger than a robin. But all of them are sturdy, powerful birds for their size, and all have long, sharp claws.

Female

Male

Unlike many other birds, male and female hawks often have the same coloring—usually some shade of brown, black, or gray. It is difficult to tell them apart from a short distance, but the female is somewhat larger than the male, and more spirited.

The cry, or call, of the hawk is unmusical to our ears, but it is often a clue to the hawk's identity. The red-tailed hawk's call sounds like the hiss of escaping steam; the broad-winged hawk utters a weak, drawn-out whistle, and the sparrow hawk chatters a rapid *killee-killee-killee.*

There are almost forty different kinds of hawks in North America. They range from the tropics to the Arctic Circle, and all over the United States. Every woodland and meadow, mountain range or coastal region may be the home of some kind of hawk. The marsh hawk loves the open bottom lands; the Cooper's hawk seeks the deep forests; the osprey and the eagle are found near rivers and lakes. Wherever there is food available, there will be at least one kind of hawk.

Hawks are birds of prey which, unlike owls, hunt during the daylight hours. They eat small animals like mice, shrews, or ground squirrels, also birds, insects, and reptiles. In winter, or whenever food is scarce, some hawks will seize chickens or small game. Many farmers and sportsmen dislike hawks for this reason. Often they try to kill every hawk they see, even though only a few kinds of hawks prey upon such creatures.

Actually, hawks are of value to us. By killing some of the millions of mice and insects that are born every year, they help maintain the balance of nature. Mice would soon overrun the orchards and fields if there were no hawks. Vultures, sometimes mistakenly called buzzards, help us keep our countryside clean by eating the dead or sick animals they find on the roads or in the fields.

All hawks are skilled fliers and most of them hunt their food from the air. Their strong wings hold them aloft for long periods while they circle high in the sky, soaring and gliding as they search the ground below them for an unwary victim.

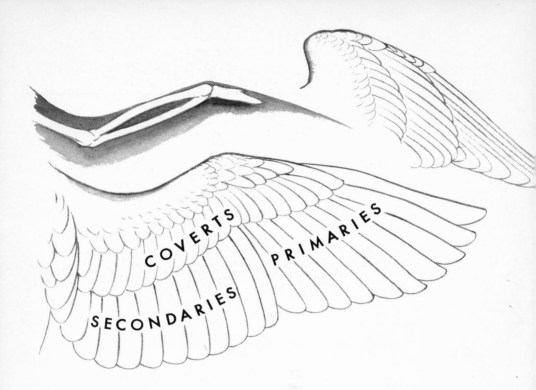

The wings of hawks are perfectly designed for soaring; that is, for gaining altitude on fully outstretched wings. Many birds are able to glide (to ride descending air currents), but most of them have to flap their wings constantly to stay aloft. This is not true of hawks. The surface of a hawk's wing is curved in such a way that the air currents passing over it actually *lift* its body. Our airplanes are built on exactly the same principle. It is the relation of the weight of the body to the curved surface of the wing that makes it possible for both a hawk and an airplane to move forward and upward on motionless, outstretched wings.

Some hawks have long, tapered wings and a long tail; these are the true falcons. The American sparrow hawk, one of our most common hawks, and the duck hawk are falcons. The group of hawks called Accipiter have short, round wings and long tails. The sharp-shinned hawk and the Cooper's hawk, both sometimes called chicken hawks, belong to this group. Hawks of the Buteo group, the slow-flying mousehawks, have stout bodies and rounded wings and tails. The red-tailed hawk, a large hawk with a wingspread of more than four feet, and the broad-winged hawk are true mouse-eating hawks.

Accipiters   Falcons   Buteos

When we see it resting on a limb, a hawk looks dumpy and sluggish. But the instant it sees some small animal below, it becomes very alert. The loose, rumpled look disappears before our eyes, and soon the hawk soars into the air above the creature for a better look. If it proves to be something it likes to eat, the hawk dives at its prey, with eyes dead ahead and wings half-closed. If it dives from high in

15

the air, it may flap its wings several times to gain additional speed, but its attack is almost soundless. Unless the victim saw the hawk leave its perch, it is usually too late for it to escape.

The duck hawk is the swiftest of all hawks. This bird dives upon its prey—usually another bird—with such speed and force that a second attack is seldom needed. It is estimated that this hawk may exceed a speed of 150 miles per hour in its dive.

The hawk's eyes, beak, and talons also add to its skill as a hunter. The first thing we notice when we watch a hawk is its piercing eyes. No one can be sure just how powerful a hawk's eyes are, but we do know that from a perch in a treetop, or while it is circling high in the sky, it can spot a little brown mouse scampering through the grass.

The eyes are large and are placed at an angle to the head. Hawks are able to see on each side as well as directly in front of them. This ability to see in two directions at once is heightened by the unusual retina in the hawk's eye, which is divided into two parts. The back part of the retina co-ordinates the eyes so they focus together; the forward part of the retina makes it possible for the hawk to focus each eye separately. One eye may be sensitive to a movement at one side of the hawk's head; the other eye may be directed at an entirely different object on the other side.

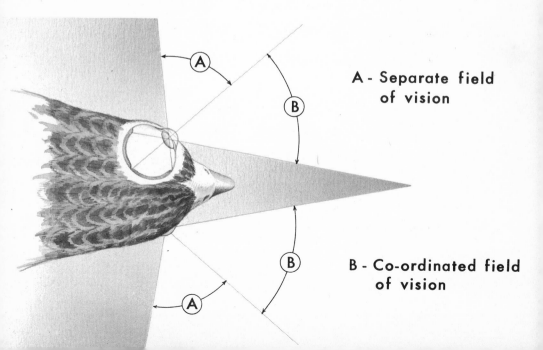

A - Separate field
of vision

B - Co-ordinated field
of vision

The eyes of a young hawk are dull gray, but they change color as the bird grows older. Some hawks have bright yellow eyes, others red, and some brown.

The "angry" look that all hawks have is caused by a strip of bone over each eye. This peculiar bone acts as a shield against the sun's rays while the hawk hunts or soars in the sky. It is not found in any other bird.

The hawk's feet are strong, and the curved claws are just right for holding its prey. A hawk's victim rarely struggles free, even when it weighs almost as much as its captor.

The tendons that control a hawk's toes are located on the outside of the bird's heel. When the hawk strikes with its feet outstretched, the toes are open. As soon as it hits its prey, its

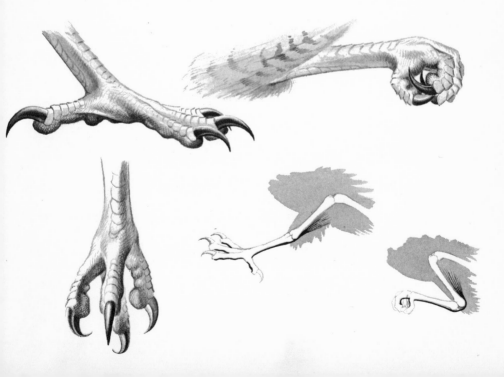

body tilts forward, automatically shortening the
tendons that close its talons. They will remain
closed until the bird straightens up. Very few
other birds use their feet to seize their food,
as hawks do, but many of them can shorten

their tendons in the same way. This is why a
perching bird does not fall from its roost while
it sleeps. As the bird grasps a limb, its body
settles forward. As long as the body is in this
position, the talons grasp and hold.

Since the hawk is a flesh eater, its beak is very sharp and powerful. As soon as a hawk seizes its prey, it flies to a nearby perch and, with one sharp twist of its beak, kills it. It may then carry it to a safer, higher perch where it can eat at its leisure. Like owls, which are also flesh eaters, hawks do not swallow their prey whole unless it is very small. They tear it into little pieces before they swallow it.

Great care must be used in handling a live hawk that is not used to human hands. Hawks can inflict deep wounds with their talons and beak. If a hawk is wounded or cornered, it will flop over on its back and fight its enemy with beak and talons. A man climbing up to a goshawk's nest was attacked by the angry bird. It

was fortunate that he was wearing a tin pan on his head to protect himself, for the hawk struck the pan twice with enough force to dent the tin.

It is difficult to get close enough to a hawk to watch its eating habits. Naturalists who have studied the food found in the stomachs of dead hawks report that each kind of hawk is apt to eat the same kind of animal or bird time after time, as long as it can find it. But hawks are able to adjust their eating habits to fit local conditions. If they cannot find their favorite food, they will eat any other small animal, bird, or reptile that is available. This is why some of the larger hawks will sometimes attack chickens or small game, even though these animals are not usually a part of their diet.

The sparrow hawk is found all over our country, Mexico, and Central America, and in parts of Canada. This attractive bird, only slightly larger than a robin, likes meadow mice and insects, but its diet varies greatly, depending on the region in which it lives. Naturally the food a sparrow hawk catches in the open country of Oklahoma is quite different from the food eaten by one living in the woods of our eastern mountains. In recent years this little hawk has often been seen in cities, feeding in parks and vacant lots. During the winter months, when insects and mice are not easy to find, the sparrow hawk will attack English sparrows.

This small falcon is very beautifully marked. The male has a russet back and tail, bluish-gray wings, and a white, buff, or rufous breast.

Although the sparrow hawk is welcome almost anywhere, this is not true of the Accipiters. The hawks in this group feed mostly on birds. Some of them are large enough to attack chickens or ducks.

The Cooper's hawk is typical of these bold and daring hawks. It is a slender, medium-sized bird with short, rounded wings and a long tail and is usually slate gray in color, with a light reddish-brown breast. Like most

hawks, it has scaly yellow legs and feet, and its tail is black. It hunts in the woodlands, flying close to the ground and darting suddenly upon any luckless bird it may find. Many times it will even pursue a bird that has flown into the underbrush for cover and drive it into the open. This hawk constantly seeks birds of all sizes as food, but it will also eat squirrels and chipmunks.

The osprey is sometimes called a fish hawk, because it eats fish. It is a large bird, attractively marked with black and white, and its eyes are yellow. Its long, narrow wings may have a wingspread of almost six feet. This hawk is an alert hunter. It flies over the water, watching for any fish that may be swimming near the surface. When it spots one it hovers for a moment and then plunges down with a great splash, sometimes diving below the surface of the water. The osprey's large, powerful feet are equipped with exceptionally long claws, and the soles of its toes are covered with sharp spines, or spicules. These enable it to hold fast to its slippery prey while carrying it off to a favorite perch in a tree to eat it.

The osprey is rarely hunted by irate farmers,

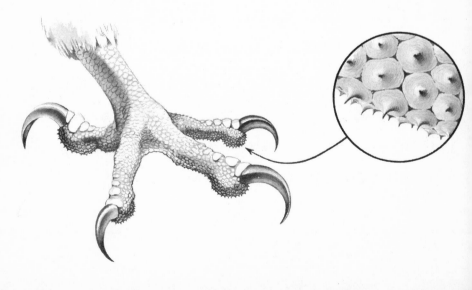

because it seldom eats anything except fish. Its peaceful life is sometimes interrupted, however, by the bald eagle, which also eats fish. If a bald eagle sees an osprey catch a nice large fish, it dives down and attacks the smaller bird until it drops the fish and flies off. The bald eagle can dive so fast that it is able to catch the fish before it reaches the water.

The marsh hawk, a harrier, is often seen gliding just above the tops of the goldenrod and cattails in low marshlands and fields. It is one of the few hawks that show a difference in color between the male and the female. The male has a bluish-gray back and a white breast; the female is brown, with markings on its buff breast. Both adult birds have a white spot just above the tail, which makes them easy to identify in the field. This hawk spends most of its life near or on the ground, often perching on a low snag or a muskrat hill. It is weak and timid for its size, and is sometimes shot just because it is an easy target. It should not be killed; it feeds almost entirely on mice, frogs, or snakes.

The Audubon's caracara is an unusual hawk
of our southern states. This long-legged bird
with black-and-white wings and tail, and a
black crown, is slow-moving compared to other
hawks. It often feeds with vultures on dead animals; it does kill some of the smaller animals.

Vultures, unlike other hawks, seldom kill their own food. Although their feet are fairly large, they are weak and the talons are not sharp. These clumsy, bald-headed birds are beautiful only when they soar high in the sky. Vultures are truly masters of flight.

Like nearly all North American birds, most hawks fly south when the leaves color in the fall. As yet, we know very little about hawk migration; only scattered records come in each year and there are no records at all for many parts of the country. We do know that, over level or slightly rolling country, hawks move in scattered flights. Often there are only two or three birds in sight at one time, all soaring lazily in the sky, as if they weren't going any place at all. They are on the move, though.

Hawks usually travel about 50 to 75 miles a day, a short distance compared to ducks and other shore birds, which cover as many as 350 miles a day. Their fondness for soaring stands the hawks in good stead when they near a mountain range. They group closely together and glide along the updrafts of wind created by the mountain ridges.

Hawks may use almost any series of hills or ridges that parallel their north-south flight. Kittatinny Ridge, in eastern Pennsylvania, is famous for its spectacular migratory flights of hawks. Because of the weather conditions and air currents along this ridge, they glide very close to its top. Each year thousands of hawks from the northeastern part of our country and Canada follow this route, soaring southward for hours with hardly a flap of their wings.

In the early 1900's, city sportsmen and hunters went out to the ridge to shoot the hawks as they passed. The needless slaughter was so great that many evenings there would be a wagonload of dead and dying hawks at the base of the cliffs. Now part of the ridge is Hawk Mountain Sanctuary, a protected area where bird lovers may study the migratory habits of hawks. An average of 500 hawks a day pass through this sanctuary each autumn, during September and October. One observer counted 4078 broad-winged hawks in a single day!

In the spring, hawks return to northern re-
gions to mate and breed their young. Their
nests are usually hard to find. They are all very
shy of man, their greatest enemy, and in order
to protect the babies they often build in high
or out-of-the-way places.

The sparrow hawk is one of the few hawks that will accept a nesting box placed by man. It is the only hawk that does not build an open nest. It likes an old flicker hole in a dead tree, or a natural cavity. It lays four to six eggs on wood chips or waste material that has collected in the hole.

Hawks' nests vary greatly in size. Most of them are constructed of twigs, securely twisted and wedged into the fork of a tree so that the nest will be safe in high winds and thunderstorms. Red-tailed hawks may use the same nest a second year. They merely add a new layer of sticks and, sometimes, a new lining to the old nest. This hawk does not try to hide its nest; it builds in the open where it can watch the surrounding countryside. If an unwelcome visitor passes by, it flies away from the nest until the intruder leaves.

Many hawks build their nests on old squirrel nests. These nests, also securely fastened in the fork of a tree, may be identified by the base of dead leaves, which are not otherwise used as nesting materials by birds.

The marsh hawk builds its nest on the ground, often right in the marshlands. The duck hawk, now growing rare, lays its eggs on some high, secluded ledge. The osprey makes its nest almost anywhere. It will nest on the ground, on a telegraph pole, in a tree, or even on an unused chimney top. Wherever it is, we may be sure the nest will be near water.

Many hawks that nest in trees have the unusual habit of keeping fresh branches of pine, hemlock, or other leaves on the rim of the nest. Broad-winged hawks are noted for always having fresh leaves on their nests. We do not know exactly why they do this. Probably the green leaves help camouflage the nest and protect it from crows or squirrels, which are always looking for a fresh egg or two to eat. The nest of the broad-winged hawk is often so poorly built that you can see the hawk's tail through it when you stand under the tree.

Vultures do not build much of a nest. They will use any natural cavity—often just an offset in a rock ledge or a small cave—in which to lay their two eggs.

Bald eagles, however, return to the same large nest each year, merely adding new layers of sticks to the old structure each spring. Some of these nests measure as much as six feet across and twelve feet deep after they have been in use for many years.

Not all hawks lay the same number of eggs. The nest of the red-tailed hawk usually contains three eggs, sometimes only two. These hawks often nest before the leaves are out in the spring, although they may have eggs as late as the end of June. The marsh hawk, like the sparrow hawk, lays from four to six eggs. The incubation period of the sparrow hawk, the bald eagle, and the marsh hawk is twenty-eight to thirty days. The sharp-shinned hawk's eggs require only twenty-one days to hatch. In most cases both adult birds share the task of incubating the eggs.

1 WEEK

2 WEEKS

It takes most of the summer for young hawks to grow a full set of feathers. They are almost naked when they hatch, but their thin, grayish down is soon replaced by a thick coat of soft, cottony feathers. Within a short time, feather

4 WEEKS

5 WEEKS

sheaths appear on the wings. When the sheaths open and peel off, the flight feathers are exposed.

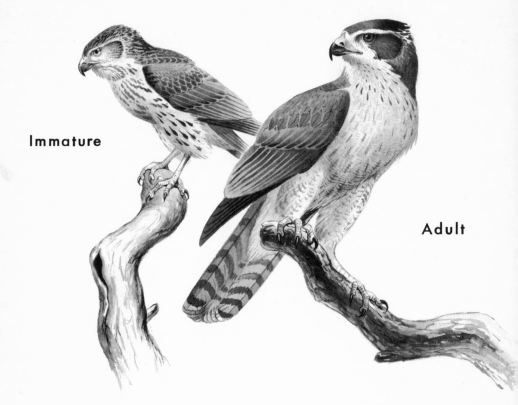

Immature

Adult

Young hawks are often not as colorful as their parents. They are usually faded brown in color, with heavily streaked breasts and dull gray eyes, which do not change color until the next year.

The markings of young hawks are often quite different from those of their parents. One of the most striking examples of this change in coloring is the bald eagle. Young bald eagles

Immature

Adult

RED-SHOULDERED HAWK

do not have white heads and tails until they are three years old. Because of this, many of them are mistaken for large hawks or vultures, and are needlessly shot.

After they leave the nest, young hawks are an easy target for hunters and larger birds of prey. It is unusual for more than two birds from a family of five to live long enough to mate and to raise a family of their own the following spring.

As soon as the eggs begin to hatch, hawks, like all bird parents, are kept busy hunting for food for their babies. Some hawks begin collecting food even before the eggs hatch. Many times I have found three or four meadow mice and parts of a squirrel tightly wedged into the rim of a red-tailed hawk's nest, ready for the hatching of the eggs. During the time they are caring for their young, hawks may become so pressed for food that they will kill birds or animals not usually included in their diet.

Some people will not go near a hawk's nest when there are babies in it, for fear of being attacked by the adult birds. It is true that the goshawk and the bald eagle may attack anyone who approaches the nest, but most hawks fly away quickly and quietly when they are disturbed, not returning for an hour or so. I have

watched several Cooper's hawk's nests and have found it almost impossible to get close enough to them to see the adult bird leave. Once I did see the female dive from the nest. When she was just a few feet from the ground, she flew swiftly into the heavy woods.

Although the hawk is a tireless hunter, it is also one of the most relentlessly hunted of all birds. Man is its chief enemy. Unfortunately, many farmers shoot any hawks they see, and some hunters also shoot them, because they think these birds destroy game.

Crows are also enemies of the hawk, although they can do it little real harm. No two wild birds dislike each other more heartily. Crows caw with malicious delight when they

see a hawk. Sometimes a whole flock will gather to dive and scream at their foe until the hawk tires of the noisy disturbance. Then it begins to circle higher and higher into the sky, leaving the crows far behind. Wheeling and soaring high above its lesser foes, the hawk is still king of the air.